Use this notebook to jot down your ideas, thoughts and musings

Copyright © 2021

Simone Laraway.

All rights reserved. This book or any portion thereof may not be reproduced or used in any manner whatsoever without the express written permission of the author except for the use of brief quotations in a book review.

Printed by KDP Amazon

First printing, 2021.

simone@thevocalbureau.com

www.thevocalbureau.com

Cover Design – Melli M Designs

THE HOLISTIC GUIDE TO COLD-CALLING

A Step-By-Step Guide To Help You Create New Business Opportunities

Simone Laraway
Founder of The Vocal Bureau

Define Yourself

- Who Are you?
- What is it that you do?
- Hopes & Dreams
- What's Your Story?
- What are your skills or talents?
- Any Awards?
- Who are your clients?

Learn New Skills

Think Outside The Box

Collaborate

Let your mind wander

Brainstorm with friends & colleagues

Research What Others Are Doing

Put pen to paper or fingers to the keys.

Network

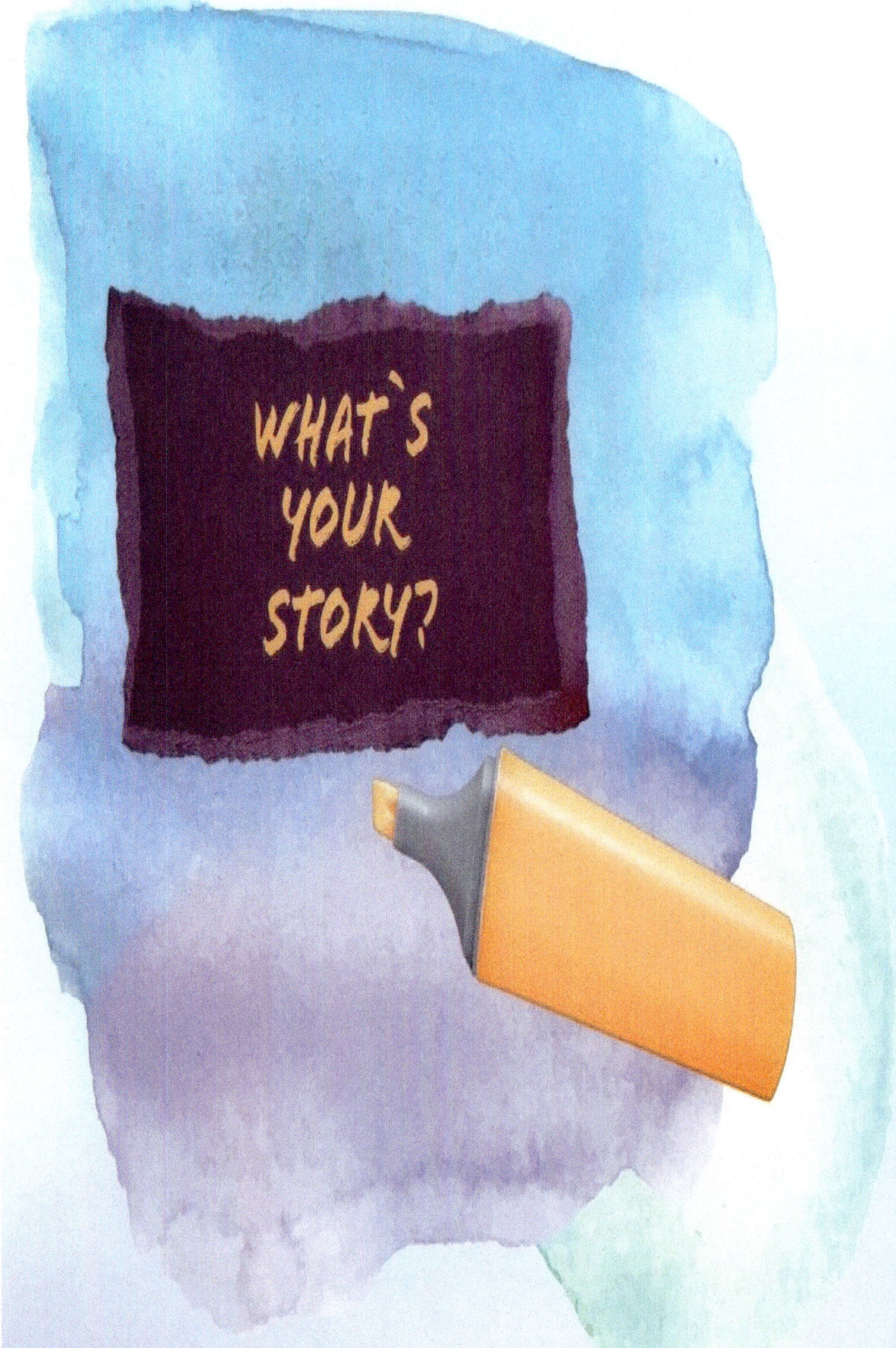
WHAT`S
YOUR
STORY?

BLOW YOUR OWN TRUMPET

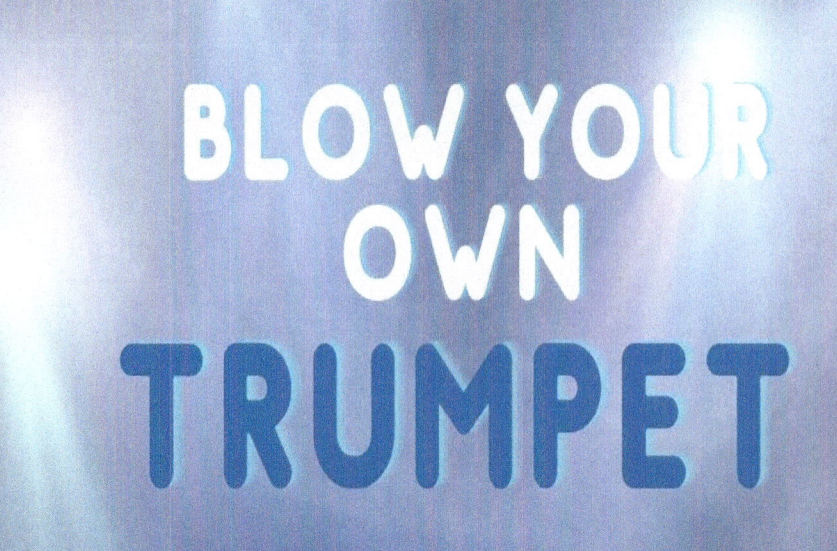

WHO?

WHO YOU GONNA CALL?

WHO?

Why are you calling?

Possible Reasons

- Set up a meeting/appointment, be it online or face to face

- Arranging a demo

- You are trying to sell a product or service

- Inviting someone to a conference or webinar

- Building brand awareness and you want to build your email list

- You are looking for the right contact name

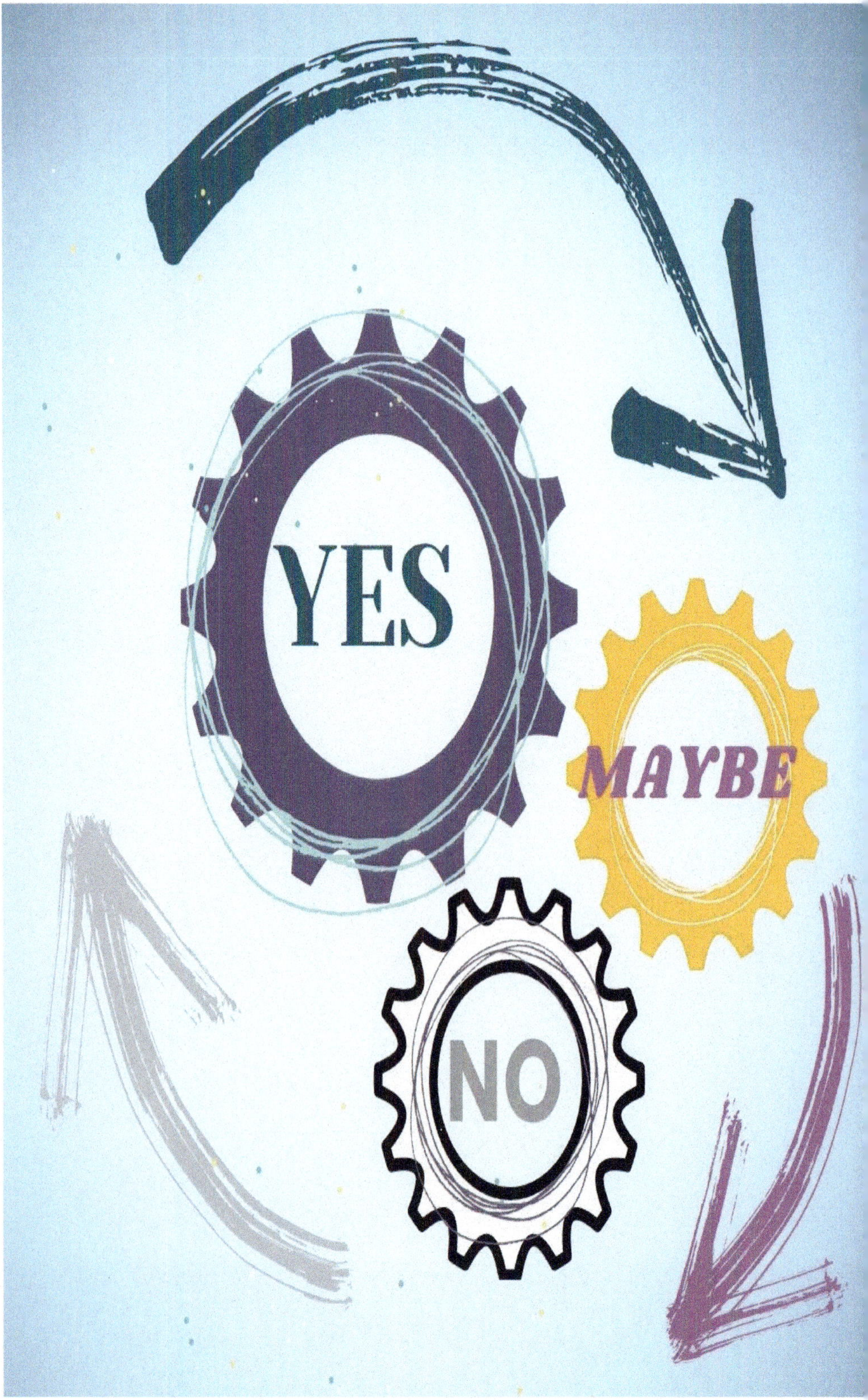
YES
MAYBE
NO

GOAL

HOTS

Warms

Cultivate

NO's and not spoken to

Cold Calls

Graphic design by Melli M Designs

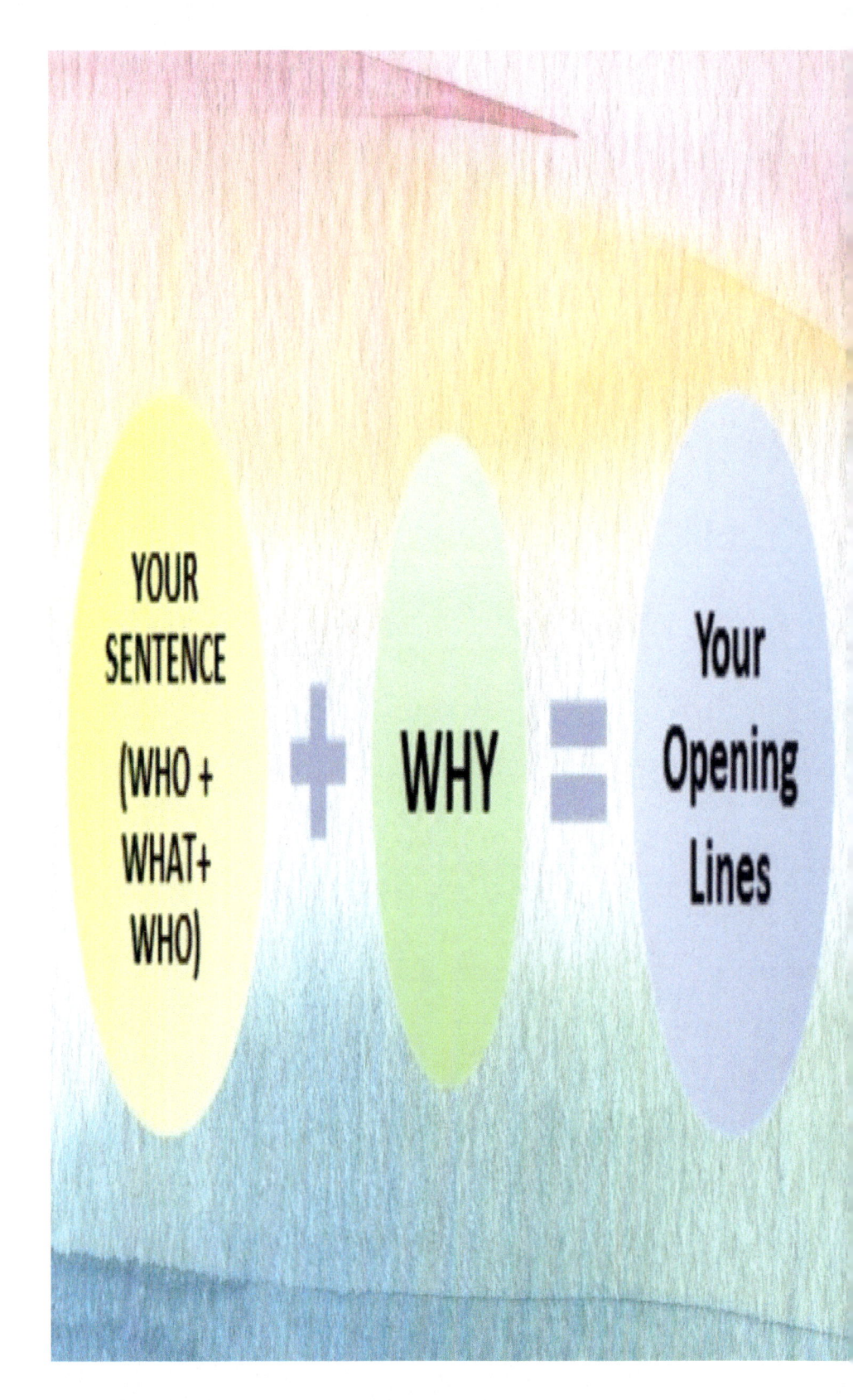

YOUR SENTENCE (WHO + WHAT+ WHO) **+** WHY **=** Your Opening Lines

SCRIPT TEMPLATE

ADDRESS:
NAME:
EMAIL:
PHONE:
WEB ADDRESS:

Good Morning/ Afternoon could I speak to

My name is

and I am calling from

We're

and work with

I was hoping to arrange

IF YES – Perfect. Can I take your email address and I will send you a diary invite (or whatever you have agreed upon) and a link to our website.

If NO/Maybe then ask open questions -

When, Why, How, What

CHALLENGE TIME!

Set your stop-watch and see how long it takes you to say your script. You're aiming for under 20 seconds but are also trying to sound relaxed!

Your Toolkit

Your kit should include the following:

- An up-to-date, well maintained and easy to navigate website

- A professional business email address

- A follow-up email template

- Examples of your work

- Quotes from clients/customers

- Links to your social media

- A rate card, if applicable

To Do List

EMAIL TEMPLATE

EMAIL EXAMPLE:

Re: Your Company name & anything you think will grab attention

Dear

Thank you for your time today *(personalise this if anything else happened on your call)*. As promised, here are further details regarding *(Your Company Name)*.

As I mentioned on the phone today, we are (**SAY WHAT YOU DO**)

I've attached examples of our work/here is a link to my work/YouTube Channel – **whatever you feel is relevant to your company and what you think would be the right thing to showcase you.**

You can also visit our website: …………………………….

(If you have any insight into the company and why you feel you can benefit them, then put that here.)

If you have any questions or would like to arrange (YOUR WHY), please do not hesitate to drop me a line or call me on (*phone number or email address. Tailor this sentence to match your* **WHY**).

I look forward to speaking again soon. (Or as promised, I will give you a call on…)

Kind regards

In your signature include any social media links, your logo, email and telephone number.

Make good calls!

LISTEN! LISTEN! LISTEN!

Vocal Care

- Voice Warm-ups

- Warm up your neck and shoulders

- Stay hydrated

- Be mindful of your posture

- Use a headset to prevent neck strain

- Steam your throat

Your Pre-Call Reminder

- Wipe the sweat from your brow!
- Database open
- Script at hand
- Email template and Toolkit ready
- Smile and keep pleasant thoughts in your head and know that it's not enough just to smile. The smile needs to come from a place or sincerity for it to colour your voice.
- Visualise that the day ahead is going to be productive
- Your website open if it inspires you.
- A pleasant work environment.
- A relaxed attitude.
- Warm-up your voice.
- Set your intention to have good conversations.
- Take breaks as and when you need them.
- Don't let rejections get you down. Just move on.
- Be diligent with your note keeping.
- Follow up with any requests immediately!
- Do not take the energy from the last call into the next one. Each call is individual.
- LISTEN, LISTEN, LISTEN
- Enjoy yourself

Happy Calling!

To Do List

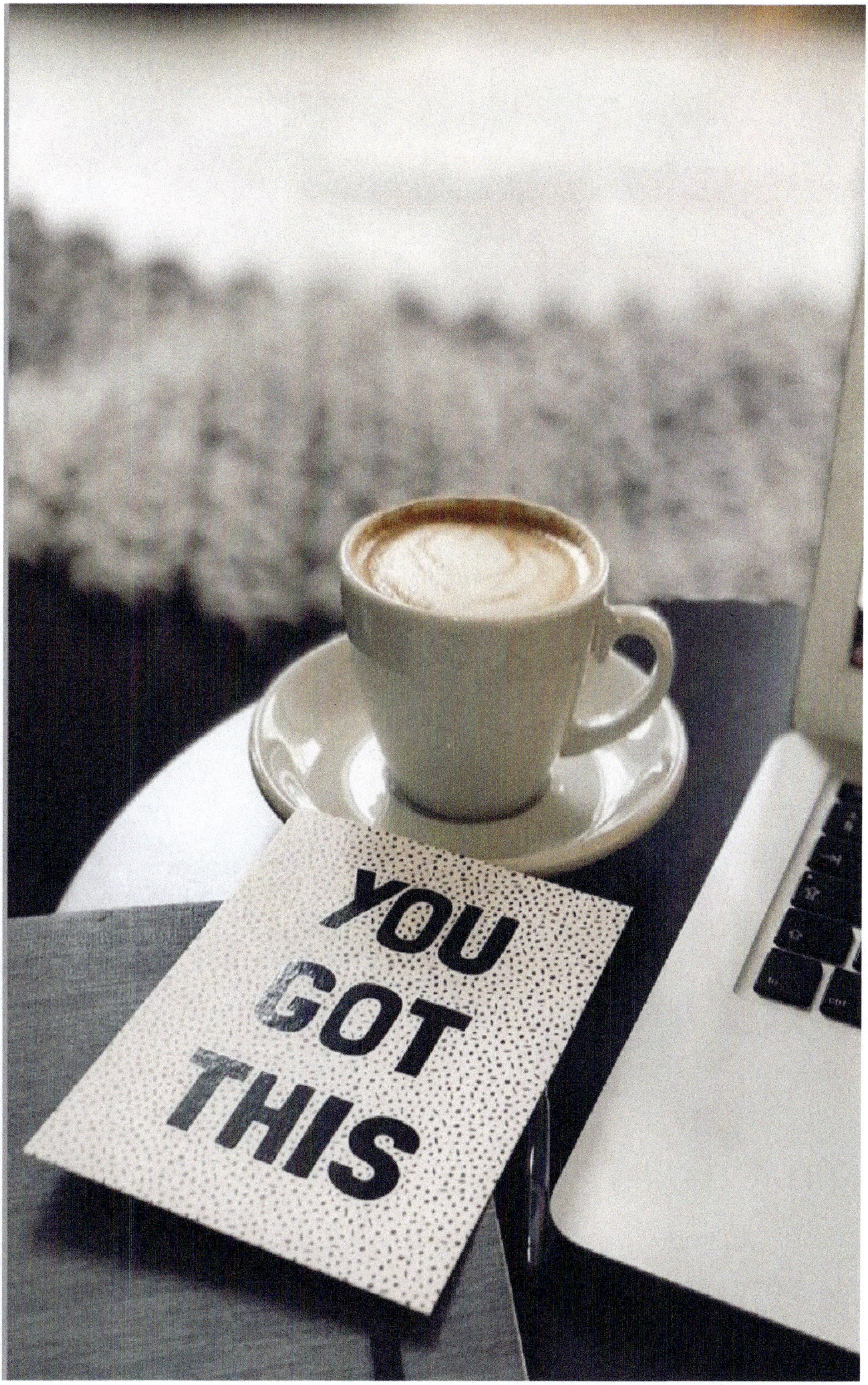
YOU
GOT
THIS

About The Author

Simone has always loved to talk and has created a path for herself centred around voice.

With a Combined Honours Degree in English Literature & Music from The University of Southampton, Postgraduate Diploma & LRAM in Vocal Studies, from The Royal Academy of Music and a VoiceGym Practitioner, she has worked as a voice coach for over 20 years.

Her cold-calling experience stemmed from running new business and marketing for The Voice Gym in Southampton. She found she loved being on the phone building relationships with potential clients.

This led to her working with companies from across the marketing services sector, both B2B & B2C. Simone has been a successful new business consultant for over 20 years.

To connect her skills and experience, The Vocal Bureau was born. She helps individuals and companies learn what to say, how to say it and whom to say it to.

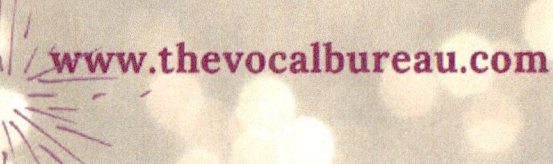

www.thevocalbureau.com

THE
HOLISTIC GUIDE
TO COLD-CALLING

A Step-By-Step Guide To Help You
Create New Business Opportunities

www.thevocalbureau.com

RESOURCES

USEFUL LINKS

The Vocal Bureau - www.thevocalbureau.com

Email me: simone@thevocalbureau.com

For Beautiful Designs –

https://www.facebook.com/MelliMDesigns

LEADS

www.electricmarketing.co.uk

Free CTPS Checker | Electric Marketing

ALF Insight | Agency New Business

www.linkedin.com

Telephone Preference Service - (ctpsonline.org.uk)

CRM SYSTEMS

www.salesforce.com

www.thehubspot.com

www.goldmine.com

www.pipedrive.com

HEALTH & WELLBEING

VoiceGym - www.voicegym.co.uk

The Complementary Medical Association
www.the-cma.org.uk

Dr Peter Glidden – MD Naturopath
https://www.riseupintohealth.com
https://riseupintohealth.com/?via=simone

The British Voice Association
https://www.britishvoiceassociation.org.uk

Yoga With Adrienne – YouTube

The Daily Om – Courses
www.dailyom.com/cgi-bin/courses/courses.cgi

Ikigai: The Japanese secret to a long and happy life - By Hector Garcia & Francesc Miralles

THE HEALING POINT: Your step-by-step guide to ketogenic wellness – By James Lilley

EQUIPMENT

Yoga Ball & Theraban – For posture and voice work

Facial Steamer

Notebooks for scribbling ideas -

www.magictreebooks.co.uk

THANK YOU FOR READING.

If you enjoyed the journey please feel free to give a big thumbs-up on Amazon.

Thank you!

Printed in Great Britain
by Amazon